W9-AFN-836

TOM RIDGWAY

Epidemics
Deadly Diseases
Throughout History

SMALLPOX

The Rosen Publishing Group, Inc.
New York

To PJR, who made sure I got all my shots.

Published in 2001 by The Rosen Publishing Group, Inc.
29 East 21st Street, New York, NY 10010

Library of Congress Cataloging-in-Publication Data

Ridgway, Tom.
Smallpox / by Tom Ridgway. — 1st ed.
        p.   cm. — (Epidemics!)
Includes bibliographical references and index.
ISBN 0-8239-3346-6 (lib. bdg.)
1. Smallpox—History—Juvenile literature. [1. Smallpox—History. 2. Diseases—History. 3. Epidemics—History.] I. Title. II. Series.
      RC183.1 .R53 2000
      616.9'12'009—dc21

                                                          00-009890

Cover image: A color-enhanced electron micrograph of smallpox (variola)

Manufactured in the United States of America

CONTENTS

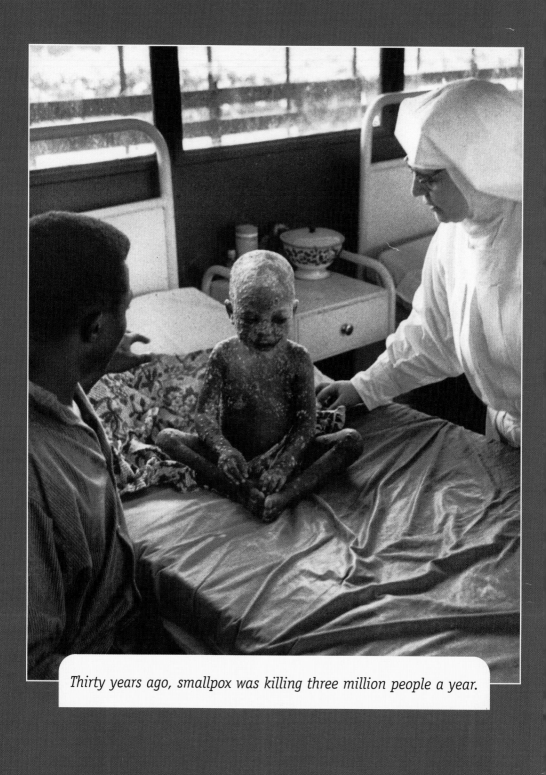

Thirty years ago, smallpox was killing three million people a year.

INTRODUCTION

How old are you? If you had been born 200 years ago, chances are you would never have made it to be so old, not with smallpox around. Only thirty years ago, smallpox was killing three million people a year—that's equal to the population of West Virginia dying every year from one disease. But relax, smallpox no longer exists—and we'll find out why later.

First, let's go back 200 years. In 1800, English historian Thomas Macaulay wrote:

Smallpox was always present, filling the churchyard with corpses, tormenting with constant fear all whom it had not yet stricken, leaving on those whose lives it spared the hideous traces of its power . . . and making the eyes and cheeks of the betrothed maiden objects of horror to the lover.

Smallpox was everywhere. It killed thousands of people in each place it struck—Boston, London, Berlin, Bombay, Cairo—and if smallpox didn't kill people, it disfigured them. Smallpox scars were bigger and deeper than chicken pox scars, and they covered the whole face. The name "smallpox" came from these scars, otherwise known as pox. To distinguish smallpox from another disease—syphilis—which was called great pox, the name smallpox came into being.

Smallpox could strike at any moment. And when it did, it spread very quickly. Take this example:

In 1972, a man returned to his home in Yugoslavia after a trip to Mecca, Saudi Arabia. He had caught smallpox. Nobody realized that it was smallpox at first because there had been no cases in the country since 1927, and he passed it on to someone else. This second man, Ljatif, a schoolteacher, got a really bad case of smallpox and was sent to the hospital. The hospital staff didn't know what he had, so they sent him to another hospital, but there they didn't know either. He eventually ended up in Belgrade, the capital of Yugoslavia.

At every hospital Ljatif stayed in he infected a new group of people; doctors say that every person with the disease infects another ten to twenty people. In the end Ljatif died—and so did thirty-four other people. But that wasn't the end. To stop the infection from spreading, the whole country was shut down. Nobody could leave their homes. All the neighboring countries closed their borders. And nearly everybody was given a new smallpox shot.

To begin with, one man had the disease, but his infection meant that 18 million people (out of a population of 21 million people) had to be given new shots. If they hadn't, many more people would have died.

To find out how smallpox started, how many people it killed, how it was destroyed, and why it might still be scary, you'll have to read on.

1

THE VIRUS GRENADE

Scientists say the smallpox virus looks like a hand grenade. It is shaped like a brick and covered with little spiky bits. Viruses are microorganisms that need to live inside the cells of a host in order to survive. For smallpox, that host was us—humans. Animals tend to have their own version of the pox. To name just a few, there's cowpox (an important one as we'll see), horsepox (it died out), sealpox, deerpox, skunkpox, peacockpox, Nile crocodilepox, kangaroopox, and insectpox (it melts the insides of caterpillars; no cure has been found yet). Smallpox is much bigger than most viruses (about 300 million of them could fit in the period at the end of this sentence). It could also lie asleep for a long time.

Scientists are amazed by the smallpox virus because it is very complicated. Viruses are generally made up of a strand of deoxyribonucleic acid, or DNA, covered by proteins that act as a kind of protective layer. (We all have DNA; it's made up of genes, the most basic parts of us.) In the smallpox virus, there are a hundred different proteins protecting a strand of DNA containing 187 genes. For a virus that means it's very, very complicated—for example, the AIDS virus has only ten genes.

How Smallpox Spreads

Smallpox was spread by people breathing it in. It entered the body and found a home in the back of the throat where it mixed with saliva. This meant that once inside the body, every time someone spoke or even breathed through his or her mouth, the person would send little "grenades" of smallpox out into the air in tiny droplets of saliva. The grenades would then hang around in the air until someone else breathed them in. Just standing next to someone in a shop or in the street would mean that you could get the disease. Once the virus was in the body, it would start to invade the body's cells. This was a smart virus, and it used the body of its host to help it spread. It would steal bits of the cell's proteins to

250 BC
Smallpox is introduced into China by the Huns.

1438
A smallpox epidemic kills 50,000 in Paris, France.

1500 BC
Smallpox probably makes the jump from an unknown animal to humans somewhere in the Nile Valley.

581
Gregory of Tours describes a smallpox epidemic in southern France.

make a tail for itself. Then, looking like a microscopic tadpole, it would start to try to get out of the cell it was in. It would bang into the cell wall and, for some reason scientists cannot explain, this would make the cell sprout little tubes. These tubes would move out from the cell until they touched another cell. Then the little tadpole would journey through the tubes and move to a new cell. And because the "tadpole" moved without actually going into the blood, the body's defenses did not know anything was wrong (antibodies, one of the body's lines of defense, are in the blood). The virus spreads when the first cell exploded and lots of smallpox viruses (without tails) were released. But even then the

1518
The first epidemic on Hispaniola— probably only a thousand people survived.

1633
Smallpox strikes the Native American population living near Plymouth Colony, Massachusetts.

1660
An estimated 40,000 Brazilian Indians are killed by smallpox.

c. 1526
Smallpox reaches the Incas in the Andes.

(continued)

antibodies were confused because these new smallpox viruses were covered in armor, which stopped the body's defenses from attacking them. And so it went, until the virus had spread all over the body.

Grim Details of the Pox

Meanwhile, you wouldn't notice anything odd until about ten to twelve days after breathing in the first virus cells. Then suddenly you would start to feel awful—a fever (your temperature could reach 104 degrees), a headache, and back and muscle pain would begin. The next step depended on which type of smallpox—major or minor—you had. The minor

1707
Smallpox arrives in Iceland and kills 18,000 out of a population of 50,000.

1719
Lady Mary Wortley Montagu inoculates her son against smallpox in Constantinople.

1721
The *Sea Horse,* a British ship, brings smallpox to Boston. Nearly 900 people are killed. Cotton Mather begins inoculation in the Americas.

1763
Sir Jeffrey Amherst gives blankets from a smallpox hospital to the Native American population.

1908
An epidemic in Rio de Janeiro kills 6,500 people.

1939
Great Britain is declared free of smallpox.

1958
Viktor Zhadanov, the minister of health from the Soviet Union, calls for an effort to rid the planet of smallpox.

1966
The World Health Organization (WHO) announces the Intensified Smallpox Eradication Programme. The aim is to eradicate smallpox in ten years.

1777
George Washington begins an inoculation program in the Revolutionary army.

1796
Edward Jenner carries out the first vaccination in Berkeley, England.

1895
Sweden is the first country in the world to be free of smallpox.

1800
Dr. Benjamin Waterhouse carries out the first vaccinations in the United States.

1972
South America is declared free of smallpox.

1979
On December 9, the WHO declares the world free of smallpox. Humanity has beaten the disease.

1993
The destruction of the last samples of the virus is delayed until 1995.

1976
India is declared smallpox free.

1999
The destruction is delayed until at least 2002.

Top: *Smallpox pustules on a person's face were a symptom of the disease.*
Bottom: *After three to four weeks, the face would be deeply scarred.*

version killed about 10 percent of the people it infected (most of those were children). The major version killed between 25 and 40 percent of those it infected (both children and adults). The next stage would come two to five days later when suddenly you would be covered in a rash. After another few days the little spots would grow into blisters, or pustules as doctors call them. (This is why the medical name for smallpox is variola—the name comes from the Latin word *varus,* meaning "pustule.") The blisters would fill with pus and then after another few days they would dry up, crack, and become scabs. After three to four weeks the scabs would fall off, leaving you with deep scars. That is, if your body managed to fight off the invaders. If it didn't, then . . .

The virus would kill you. Scientists, even after years of study, are still not sure exactly how it killed people (that's why they never found a cure), but most of the time people's lungs stopped working or they had a heart attack. In the most severe cases, this is what happened: Before the first rash appeared, the inside of your body would start to bleed. The virus attacked the membranes—sheets of proteins that make up the walls of cells inside your body. There are membranes all over the body—in the eyes, lungs, liver, kidneys, heart, intestines, reproductive organs. The virus's attack destroyed these membranes and your insides would bleed and eventually collapse. Then your skin would turn dark red or even black. As your body fell apart from the inside, you would be in the most excruciating pain—and then you would die.

Did you know that the virus could be passed on if the victim was already dead? Well, remember those scabs? The virus was encased in the scabs until it was near a new victim, and then it would strike again. If the scabs found themselves in a place that wasn't too hot or too light, the virus inside could last for as long as a year. And with the most severe form of smallpox, where there was no time for scabs to form, the virus hid in the blood, which would leave your body through your eyes, your nose, or your mouth.

Now that we know how smallpox attacked people, let's see how it came about and where it went after its arrival.

2

COWS, CAMELS, AND DEATH

All of the diseases that have spread around the world and have killed millions of people came from animals—flu (pigs and ducks), tuberculosis (cattle), malaria (birds), and measles (cattle). Smallpox is no exception. Historians and scientists think that the disease first jumped from cows or maybe from camels around 3,500 years ago—around the time when farmers began to settle down into villages and later towns and cities. It was around this time that people came into close contact with animals such as cows, goats, sheep, and horses, which allowed germs to jump from the animals to humans. This probably happened in one of three places: the Nile Valley in Egypt, Mesopotamia (an area between the Tigris and Euphrates rivers, now in Iraq), or somewhere in India.

One of the first pieces of possible evidence of smallpox comes from Egypt. In 1157 BC, the pharaoh of Egypt, Ramses V, died when he was thirty, and as was usual for the pharaohs, his body was mummified. When archaeologists found the body and unwrapped it from its cloth binding thousands of years later, they found that the pharaoh's face, neck, and arms were covered in large pustules. Scientists say that they cannot be completely sure that Ramses V died of smallpox, but those pustules certainly make it appear so.

Large pustules on the mummified head of Ramses V indicate that the pharaoh may have died of smallpox.

Later on, smallpox spread to India and China. People from the Fertile Crescent (as part of the Middle East was known) used to trade goods with the Indians and Chinese, which probably is how the disease spread. We know that smallpox arrived early in India because Hinduism (the main religion in India) has a goddess of smallpox.

Sitala means the "cool one." This goddess is usually shown holding a brush to sweep the disease along in one hand and a pot of cold water to cool down sufferers in the other. On Sitala's day, people would eat only cold food and drink cold liquids so that they did not annoy the goddess.

Between AD 165 and 180, a massive epidemic spread through Rome and its empire. It is believed to have killed between 3.5 and 7 million people—out of a world population of around 200 million—including the Roman emperor, Marcus Aurelius. But the Plague of Antoninus, as historians call it, is problematic because some historians say it was smallpox while others say it was measles. However, in the ninth century, Al-Rhazi, a doctor in Baghdad who lived between 850 and 923, wrote *A Treatise on Smallpox and Measles*. Al-Rhazi was the first person to note that smallpox and measles were two separate diseases, so after the publication of his work, it became easier to identify an epidemic of smallpox.

When a disease is permanently in a society or a community, it is called endemic. The "demic" part of the word comes from *demos*, the Greek word for "people." It means that the disease is native; it lives with the people. But when a disease comes and goes, it is called epidemic. *Epi* means "upon" in Greek, so "epidemic" means literally "upon people"—it is not native to them or their communities. (And don't forget pandemics. *Pan* means "all" in Greek, so pandemics are epidemics that don't just stay in one community but move across whole countries or even the whole world—as the flu pandemic of 1917 did.)

The Spread of Smallpox Continues

Between the eleventh and fourteenth centuries, many Christians from Europe went to the Holy Land to try to win back Jerusalem from the Muslims. While there, many caught smallpox and then spread it to populations all over the continent of Europe. In 1314, Prince John, a son of Edward II of England, fell ill with smallpox—the disease had spread that far north. He survived, unlike the king of Burma, Thadominbya, who was killed by the disease in 1368. When Christopher Columbus arrived in what he called Hispaniola—now known as the Dominican Republic and Haiti—in 1492, there were a million native people living on the island. By 1620, there were none. When the Spanish first arrived on the American continent in 1519, there were approximately 100 million people living in Mexico and Central and South America; by 1620, there were only 1.6 million.

How did all of those people die? One reason was that the Spanish forced the native populations into slavery and stopped them from farming so that they starved. The Spanish also killed thousands outright. But disease was the greatest killer of all. The native people of Central and South America didn't have a chance. In Europe, the Middle East, and Asia, there were lots of animals people could domesticate— cows, horses, sheep, goats, pigs, ducks, and chickens. But in the Americas there were only five. In the south of what is now the United States, there was the turkey; in the Andes, there were the guinea pig and the llama; in tropical South America, there was the muscovy duck; and throughout the continent, there were dogs. These were not the most useful animals. Guinea pigs are cute, but they're hopeless at pulling plows. This meant that the population of the Americas never had as close contact with animals as the people back in Europe, the Middle East, and Asia—which meant that any viruses these animals might have carried never really had the chance to jump over into humans.

Hernando Cortez's soldiers brought smallpox to the New World, where it killed a quarter of the Aztec population, including the emperor, Montezuma.

The New World Gets the Pox

However, when Columbus landed on Hispaniola, he and his crew brought many germs with them. Unfortunately, these germs were new to the native population. Smallpox didn't arrive with Columbus on Hispaniola, but it finally did in 1518. From 1492 to its arrival in 1518, over 300,000 of the native population had already died from other diseases and from murder, but for the survivors smallpox would be the end. It attacked the population so badly that a Spanish colonialist on the island estimated that only 1,000 were left afterward. (And, as we noted, by 1620 there was not a single one.)

Hernando Cortez was a mercenary soldier (called a *conquistador* in Spanish). He had heard about a fabulous city full of treasure in the middle of what is now Mexico, so he decided to find it and see if he could get rich. In 1519, he landed in Mexico and marched toward the capital of the Aztec Empire, Tenochtitlán. When he arrived, he was welcomed as a returning god by the Aztec leader, Montezuma, who Cortez promptly captured. In 1520, Cortez was forced to return to the coast to stop another group of Spaniards arriving in his newly found city. Somehow, one of Cortez's soldiers became infected with smallpox. When Cortez returned to Tenochtitlán, the Aztecs had risen up against the Spanish and the conquistador was forced to withdraw with his troops. But he left smallpox behind. The disease started to kill the Aztecs, and soon a quarter of the population was dead—including the emperor. When Cortez returned, he was easily able to beat the remaining Aztecs. Cortez had beaten an empire—but only with the help of smallpox.

The disease then started to spread. It went south, crossing through Guatemala and the rest of Central America, into South America and toward the Incas, whose great empire was centered in the Andes Mountains. Smallpox reached them in 1526 and killed their emperor, Huayna Capac, and most of the court. It then proceeded to kill Capac's heir, Ninan Cuyuchi. This caused a civil war to break out over who would be the next emperor. On one side, there was Atahuallpa; on the other, his brother, Huascar. When a Spanish conquistador, Francisco Pizarro, arrived one day in 1532 with only 168 soldiers, he found an empire led by the victor, Atahuallpa, much weakened by smallpox and the war. Pizarro immediately took Atahuallpa prisoner and demanded a ransom. Even today it's probably the biggest ransom ever demanded—enough gold to fill a room twenty-two feet long, seventeen feet wide, and eight feet high! But Pizarro did not honor his side of the bargain, and after he had received his gold, he killed

The spread of smallpox to South America weakened the Inca Empire, aiding Francisco Pizarro in his conquest.

Atahuallpa anyway. Another empire had fallen with the help of smallpox.

One of the ways that the Spanish justified their conquest was by converting the local people to Christianity. When Cortez returned to Tenochtitlán, he was joined by some Aztecs who saw smallpox as punishment from the Spanish (Christian) god. If a god was so strong that it could wipe out all these people, then it must be stronger than the gods they had worshiped up to that point. It also convinced the Spanish that they were doing the right thing—that God was on their side. So smallpox didn't just destroy the lives of the Aztecs, it also destroyed their history, their culture, and their religion.

In 1633, William Wood, a settler in what is now Massachusetts, witnessed an epidemic spread through the Native Americans who lived near the Plymouth colony. The settlers had been in conflict with the native population, and Wood wrote that the "Lord put an end to this quarrel by smiting them with smallpox. Thus did the Lord allay their quarrelsome spirit and make room for the following part of his army." Once smallpox arrived in North America, it decimated Native American populations—just as it had done in Central and South America. When Hernando de Soto explored the Mississippi Valley in 1540, he found villages and encampments completely deserted—smallpox had arrived there before him. But for the most part it cannot be said that the Spanish deliberately introduced the disease—unlike one British soldier.

Biological Warfare

In 1763, Lord Jeffrey Amherst, the commander of the British forces in North America, wanted to stop Native Americans from attacking his troops. He had an idea and wrote to one of his commanders:

Could it not be contrived to send the Small Pox among those disaffected tribes of Indians? We must on this occasion use every stratagem in our power to reduce them.

A meeting was arranged between the British and tribal chiefs at Fort Pitt near Pittsburgh. The British handed over blankets that had been used by patients in the fort's smallpox hospital. It is not known whether the tactic worked, but it is the first example in history of deliberate biological warfare—using disease to fight war.

When soldiers were not spreading smallpox across North America, it was being spread by traders and trappers. As late as the nineteenth century, smallpox was coming across virgin populations (as populations with no exposure to a disease are called). In 1837, a steamboat travelling up the Mississippi River from St. Louis encountered the Mandan, a Great Plains tribe. The boat was carrying two people infected by small-pox. They infected the tribe, and in two weeks 2,000 Mandans were reduced to 40.

But if everyone knew that smallpox was such a killer, how come nobody was doing anything to try to stop it? They were. In fact, they had been for many centuries, as we shall see.

Giving Yourself a Disease

Lady Mary Wortley Montagu was the wife of the British ambassador to the Sublime Porte, the Ottoman court in Constantinople. While living in the city (now called Istanbul) in 1717, she heard about a technique that could stop smallpox. She wrote in a letter that "every year thousands of people undergo this operation" and that it had been done for hundreds of years. Lady Mary had found out about inoculation. Lady Mary was fascinated by the procedure because she had suffered from the disease as a young woman. She had lost her eyebrows and ended up being heavily scarred. Also, her brother had died of the disease.

Inoculation was based on the fact that if you had the disease once you could not get it again. (In England, servants with smallpox scars were in demand precisely because of this fact.) The process was simple: You got someone to give you variola minor, you became sick and were quarantined until the disease passed, and then you knew you were protected against a more serious strain. What Lady Mary discovered was not a new process. This technique was known all over North Africa, the Middle East, Persia (now Iran), and India. In China, powdered smallpox scabs were blown up a person's nose to inoculate him or her—a technique said to have been introduced by a wandering wise man from India in the eleventh century. Inoculation was not risk-free. French mathematicians in the 1760s calculated that there was a 1-in-7 chance of dying from smallpox caught naturally or a 1-in-200 chance of catching a deadly form of the disease through inoculation. Nonetheless, in 1719, Lady Mary had her six-year-old son inoculated. His arm was scratched, and powdered scab or liquid from a pustule was placed in the wound. He recovered without problems. When Lady Mary got back to England, another smallpox epidemic hit London. This time she decided to have her daughter inoculated. The procedure was carried out successfully and was publicized in the newspapers.

The Royal Seal of Approval

The English royal family became interested in the technique of inoculation. In 1700, Queen Anne's son and heir had died of smallpox, and Caroline, the Princess of Wales, did not want her children to succumb to the disease. But before putting what could be a deadly disease into members of royalty, a few tests had to be made. Six prisoners who were going to be executed were given a deal: If they agreed to be inoculated and survived the experiment, they would be allowed to walk free. They agreed, and the inoculations were carried out by Lady Mary's doctor, Charles Maitland, in front of the royal doctor, Sir Hans Sloane, and twenty-six others. All the prisoners survived and were released. The royal family still wasn't sure, so they had five orphan boys inoculated. They, too, all survived, and finally Princess Caroline had her two daughters inoculated.

Once the procedure had received the royal seal of approval, it spread across the country and across the

Atlantic to the colonies in North America. (In Europe, it did not really catch on at first. In France, for example, it took the death of the French king, Louis XV, from smallpox in 1774 before the process really became popular.)

In 1721, an epidemic broke out in Boston. A clergyman named Cotton Mather had heard about inoculation—from England and also from his African slave, Onesimus. He delivered a sermon calling all doctors in the city to start inoculating people. Only one, Zabdiel Boylston, was willing to try the procedure, and so on June 26, 1721, the doctor inoculated Mather's son Thomas and two slaves, Jack and Jackey. The technique caused a huge scandal in Boston. Some people thought it was against God's wishes, others thought it ridiculous to deliberately give yourself the disease. But Mather kept count, and his figures proved that inoculation was a much safer method of going about things than just letting nature take its course. At the end of the epidemic, 6 of the 244 inoculated people had died (2.5 percent), while 844 of the 5,980 (or 14 percent) who acquired the disease naturally had died.

To the Colonies and Beyond

These kinds of figures caused the procedure to spread outside of Boston—to New York, Philadelphia, and Charleston. It also gained some important supporters,

such as Benjamin Franklin and George Washington. In 1766, smallpox was one of the reasons why the Americans did not beat the British at Quebec, and Washington (who had caught smallpox and carried its scars) learned his lesson. During the American War of Independence, which began in 1776, he started an inoculation program. On March 12, 1777, he wrote to his commanders:

> You are hereby required to send me an exact return of your Regiment, and to send those recruits who have had the smallpox to join the Army. Those who have not, are to be sent to Philadelphia, to be inoculated under the direction of the commanding Officer of the City.

George Washington, himself a survivor of smallpox, started an inoculation program for his troops.

Washington's program worked. His army never suffered another epidemic of smallpox—and he beat the

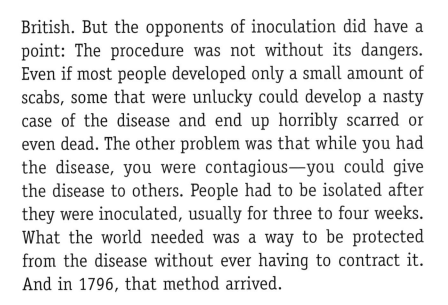

British. But the opponents of inoculation did have a point: The procedure was not without its dangers. Even if most people developed only a small amount of scabs, some that were unlucky could develop a nasty case of the disease and end up horribly scarred or even dead. The other problem was that while you had the disease, you were contagious—you could give the disease to others. People had to be isolated after they were inoculated, usually for three to four weeks. What the world needed was a way to be protected from the disease without ever having to contract it. And in 1796, that method arrived.

3

MORE COWS AND A DOCTOR

You've probably had many shots in your life: maybe polio, tuberculosis, or flu. And each time you've felt the needle go into your arm you have probably wondered who came up with this horrible procedure. However, without shots, you probably wouldn't be here today.

So how does it work? Remember the antibodies, those microscopic proteins? Well, when something strange enters the cells of your body, the cells react and call in the antibodies. There are different antibodies for different viruses and bacteria. Their job is to neutralize the invader by chemically absorbing it, destroying it, and stopping it doing any harm. (Antibodies are helped by special white blood cells, too.) If the invader has never been met before, the antibodies must work out a way to correctly destroy it. And this must be done quickly because as we have seen, the invader can multiply and multiply until there are too many invaders for the antibodies to deal with.

When you get a shot, it's like giving your body an early warning system. The vaccine sensitizes (as scientists call it) the antibodies so that if they ever meet the invader again, they know exactly what to do—they don't have to work it out. That's what inoculation did. But the really clever thing about vaccination is that it sensitizes the body's defenses with a type of virus, say cowpox, that is similar to the real target, say smallpox, but that doesn't make you really ill. Think of it this way. You and your family move, which means you have to go to a new school. Because you're a good student, you would never think of being late for school. So before the first day, you decide to walk to your new school to find out how long it will take you. You get a bit lost and take a left instead of a right and then a right instead of going straight—and you end up in the wrong place. You retrace your steps and start all over again. After a few tries, you work out the way and discover that it takes exactly eleven minutes. Now on the first day of school, you won't be late because you know exactly how long it takes to get there.

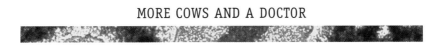

As Edward Jenner discovered (see page 36) in 1796, a vaccine is like a route map and textbook for an anti-body—it shows it how to get where it's needed and what to do when it gets there. The amazing thing about Jenner's discovery was that he didn't know any of this. He did not know what caused smallpox (viruses weren't known about then), how it was spread, or how the body reacted to and protected against disease. He just saw what seemed like a natural way of protecting people—and followed his nose.

Vaccination Rules

Vaccination began to spread around the world. In 1805, Napoleon, the leader of France, vaccinated everybody in his army (smallpox was especially dangerous to armies because there were always lots of people close to each other). Napoleon was so impressed by Jenner's discovery that when Jenner wrote to him to ask that he release two of the doctor's friends who had been captured (Britain and France were at war at the time), Napoleon immediately freed them with the words, "Ah, Jenner, we can't refuse that man anything!" By 1805, doctors in Khiatka, near Russia's border with China, were vaccinating; by 1812, merchants were distributing copies of Jenner's book to people in Samarkand in what is today Uzbekistan. Between 1808 and 1811, 1.7 million people were

Edward Jenner was born on May 17, 1749, in a small village called Berkeley, in Gloucestershire, England. His parents both died when he was five and he was brought up by his elder brother. When he was thirteen, he became an apprentice to a doctor in his hometown. Eight years later, he went to London to study with a famous doctor of the day, John Hunter. After two years in London, he turned down the chance to go on an expedition to Australia and decided to return to Berkeley.

He settled down as the local doctor, and in his spare time he studied the habits of cuckoo birds. (He was the first person to notice that cuckoos steal the nests of other birds.) But smallpox was one subject that particularly fascinated him. He remembered hearing as a child that milkmaids (the women who milked cows before there were machines to do it) often said that they could never got smallpox because they had been infected by cowpox. Jenner thought about this and decided to try an experiment. All he needed was a new case of cowpox to break out. In May 1796, a milkmaid named Sarah Nelmes caught the disease, and on May 14, Jenner took some of the pus from her blisters. He had found an eight-year-old boy named James Phipps to act as a guinea pig. He made a small wound in James's arm into which he introduced the cowpox matter he had taken from Sarah. James then developed cowpox. Next came the really important part for Jenner. On July 1, he inoculated James. (Jenner was, and still is, accused of being unethical by giving James smallpox. But this isn't fair—all he did was inoculate him, something he would have undergone anyway.) After the inoculation, James showed no signs of smallpox.

The old stories about cowpox protecting against smallpox were true!

Jenner sent his results to the Royal Society, a group in London made up of all the famous scientists of the day. But the report he wrote was rejected. Undeterred, he carried on with the experiments, and then, in 1798, wrote another report that he published himself. It was called *An Inquiry into the Causes and Effects of Variolae Vaccinae, a Disease, Discovered in some of the Western Counties of England, particularly Gloucestershire, and known by the Name of Cow Pox.* In the book, he called the pus he had taken from Sarah Nelmes "vaccine," which means 'from a cow' in Latin. And he called the whole process vaccination, which is now the word for all shots, even if they don't come from cows.

At first people were wary of vaccination. It seemed strange to introduce pus from cows into people—indeed some eminent doctors opposed to Jenner said that vaccination would turn people into cows! But most people saw that vaccination was a good thing, and Jenner's work quickly

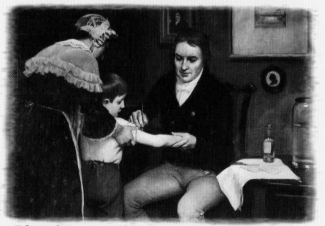

(text continued on page 40)

Edward Jenner administering an inoculation.

People were wary of Edward Jenner's vaccine. Even some eminent doctors thought that vaccination would turn people into cows!

started to spread. But there were problems. The pus from the cowpox had to be 'harvested' at just the right moment or it wouldn't be strong enough. Some doctors mixed cowpox and smallpox itself (it is said that one of Jenner's most bitter enemies deliberately contaminated a batch of cowpox with smallpox to ruin Jenner's reputation). But even with these problems, Jenner managed to win over the king and queen, and by 1801, 100,000 people in England had been vaccinated. In 1802, the doctor was awarded £10,000 by the British Parliament to thank him for his work.

vaccinated in France; and in Russia, about 2 million people had been vaccinated by 1814.

But there was one problem. How to produce the vaccine? Cowpox was quite a rare disease, and it could be difficult to find cases. Jenner's idea, which became the leading one for years to come, was called the arm-to-arm technique. One person would be vaccinated, and the pus in the cowpox blisters produced would be taken and used to vaccinate the next person. In 1804, Don Francisco Xavier Balmis set out from Spain on a vaccination mission to the Americas. With him were twenty-two orphan boys, none of whom had ever had smallpox or been vaccinated. Before they set out, one boy was vaccinated. His blisters were used to vaccinate the next, and so on. The boys were used as a human vaccination

chain all the way to the Americas. But there was one problem with this method, and it became one of the arguments used by vaccination's opponents. If the person vaccinated already had a disease, say syphilis, then this disease was passed on with the vaccination. This final problem, however, was solved when Italian scientists started to grow the vaccine directly in cows. Small wounds were made in the sides of cows, cowpox matter inserted (just like for humans), and blisters were left to grow. Then the blisters were harvested and, sadly, the cows killed.

In the United States, the technique of vaccination was first spread by a Boston doctor named Benjamin Waterhouse. In July 1800, he received some vaccine from England and immediately used it on four of his children and three of his servants. In May 1801, he sent some vaccine to New York, and vaccination was immediately started. In January 1802, a special center was set up in the city to provide free vaccination to the poor (who were more at risk because they generally lived in crowded and dirty conditions). President Thomas Jefferson became very interested in vaccination, starting programs in Washington, Baltimore, and Philadelphia. He vaccinated eighteen members of his own family, some of his neighbors, and in December 1801, he vaccinated Chief Little Turtle and his warriors when they visited Washington, DC.

Vaccination was soon practiced all over the world (it had reached Southeast Asia with Don Francisco) and some countries started to make it compulsory for their citizens. First came parts of Germany in 1807, and then Denmark in 1810. Great Britain introduced compulsory vaccination against smallpox (and at the same time outlawed inoculation) in 1853. The following year in Britain, 400,000 people were vaccinated.

Thomas Jefferson vaccinated eighteen members of his own family with the smallpox vaccine.

On January 25, 1823, Edward Jenner collapsed in his library in Berkeley and died the next day. He was buried in the local church next to his wife. In 1802, he had written about vaccination that "the annihilation of the small pox, the most dreadful scourge of the human species, must be the final result of this practice." It would take another 156 years after his death for this to happen, but he was right—smallpox's days were numbered.

4

THE WORLD HAS HAD ENOUGH

Despite the spread of vaccination around the world, smallpox continued to kill millions of people every year. In 1895, Sweden became the first country in the world to declare that it was free of smallpox; in 1899, it was followed by Puerto Rico. But things were slower in the United States, and smallpox kept returning. For example, in 1922, the disease killed 791 people. However, a new drive was launched to get everybody vaccinated and between 1948 and 1965 only one person died of the disease. In fact, by 1967 the disease had disappeared from North America and Europe. But on the other continents it was still infecting lots of people— 10 to 15 million people a year.

The World Health Organization (WHO), founded in 1948, is part of the United Nations and works to improve the general health of the world and also to coordinate attempts to eradicate communicable diseases such as polio and smallpox. In 1958, Viktor Zhadanov, the minister of health from the Soviet Union, spoke at the WHO's annual meeting. He suggested that the world try to eradicate smallpox. Eradicate a disease completely? As with vaccination, people were skeptical to begin with: It had never been done! How could you vaccinate the whole world? But just as with vaccination, the idea slowly took hold.

How to Rid the World of a Disease

The real problem with the idea lay not with the world's determination, but in the equipment it had to work with. Vaccine came in a liquid form that degraded, or broke down, quickly. It had to be used within eighteen hours or it just didn't work. That was fine in the United States or in Europe, where there were lots of modern, well-equipped hospitals. But half of the world's smallpox cases were happening in India, where travel was more difficult and where there were fewer well-equipped hospitals. This meant that vaccine was often lost and wasted. Then a laboratory in London found a new way to make the vaccine cheaply and in a way that allowed it to last for much longer. Freeze-dried vaccine was invented. Freeze-drying is done by freezing something, then placing it in a vacuum where the ice is sucked out—thus removing all the water. This creates a very stable product and all you need to do is add some water and things are back to how they were. (Instant coffee is freeze-dried, and astronauts eat freeze-dried food in space.) With freeze-dried vaccine, it was possible to keep the vaccine for much longer periods without having to worry about it not working.

The next technical achievement was to make a needle that could be easily and quickly used. A new type of needle was soon invented in the United States. It looked like a fork with two prongs, with a piece of wire between the two prongs. The right amount of vaccine was held between the two points and the wire. The needle was then jabbed into a person's skin, puncturing it and letting the vaccine enter the small wound. The needle was good because it could be reused about 200 times (after being sterilized of course) and somebody with no medical training could use it. With the new vaccine and needle in place, things were ready to go—in 1966, the WHO announced the Intensified Smallpox Eradication Programme. Its aim was to eradicate smallpox from the planet in ten years. (They decided on ten years after President Kennedy had promised to put a man on the moon within ten years—and succeeded.) An American, D. H. Henderson, was put in charge of the program. At first the idea was to vaccinate everybody on the planet, but as you can imagine, this proved difficult to do—especially in the crowded cities of India and Bangladesh.

A new idea was tried after an outbreak in Nigeria. Over 90 percent of the population had been vaccinated in the country, but smallpox broke out in a religious group that had refused vaccination. The WHO workers were short of vaccine, so instead of simply vaccinating everybody, they decided to find where each new outbreak happened. They would rush to that location and vaccinate everybody in the village. The people with the disease were isolated from everyone else and nobody was allowed to leave the village until the outbreak had died down. While the village was isolated, health workers then went to all the villages nearby to look for anyone with symptoms of the disease. Then they vaccinated those people. This was called the surveillance-containment strategy.

Breaking the Chain

As we have seen, infection works in a chain—one person gets the disease and passes it to more people who pass it to more people, etc. But if you stop people

Bangladesh was one of the last places on Earth where people contracted smallpox naturally.

passing it on to other people, then you can break the chain. And as we said, smallpox was a clever virus, but it had a fatal flaw—it could live only in humans. If everybody was vaccinated or isolated, the virus died out. This surveillance-containment method was very effective in breaking the chain of infection (and it was cheaper because it involved vaccinating fewer people). It soon became the method used all over the world, especially in India, where the smallpox eradication program employed 152,000 Indian health workers and 230 WHO personnel. The program was successful. In 1953, there were 253,322 cases of smallpox in India; by 1975, the number of cases had dropped to 1,436; and by 1976, there was not a single one.

South America was free of the disease by the end of 1972; at the end of the next year, it was found only in the Indian subcontinent and southern and eastern Africa. But with constant effort, the WHO kept fighting the disease, eradicating it in all countries until there was just one place left: Bangladesh. On October 16, 1975, a three-year-old Bangladeshi girl named Rahima Banu, broke out in a rash—she had contracted variola major, the strong form of the disease. She was quickly isolated and managed to recover. And she became famous: She was the last person ever to contract variola major naturally. Two years later, a cook in Somalia named Ali Maow Maalin got variola minor (he hadn't been vaccinated). He, too, recovered, and he became the last person to contract the mild form. Just over its ten-year time limit, it seemed that the program had managed what had once seemed impossible—humanity had at last beaten smallpox.

To be sure, the World Health Organization waited two years after Maalin's outbreak before officially declaring, on December 9, 1979, that smallpox was dead. Jenner had been right. Before its eradication, smallpox had killed around 300 million people in the twentieth century. The smallpox eradication program cost $313 million.

Aren't you glad they spent the money?

5

THE VIRUS IS OUT THERE

Smallpox may have been eradicated—but it still exists. If you wanted to get your hands on some, there are two places to start: the Centers for Disease Control in Atlanta, Georgia, or the Russian State Research Center of Virology and Biotechnology, near Novosibirsk in Siberia. (This place is also known by the James Bond–sounding name, Vector.) These two places hold the virus for research purposes and, despite the fact that it is held under very tight security, some scientists are worried.

When smallpox was eradicated, the remaining samples were sent either to the CDC in Atlanta or to the Soviet Union. (Great Britain sent its remaining viruses to Atlanta in 1983.) In 1972, the Soviet Union, the United States, and Great

The Centers for Disease Control in Atlanta is one of the few places that has samples of the smallpox virus.

Britain signed the Biological and Toxin Weapons Convention, which banned any further research into biological weapons and promised never to use them. (Now 140 other countries have signed.) But according to scientists who worked in the Soviet Union and who now live in the West, the Soviet research program carried on regardless. The Soviet Union collapsed in 1991, and many of these scientists left the country because they weren't paid or they lost their jobs. Experts think that some of them may have taken smallpox samples with them. It is believed that there are a lot more countries holding the smallpox virus than simply the United States and Russia. The U.S. government has a list of countries it believes have the smallpox virus. They keep the list secret, but it is thought to include the following countries: China, India, Pakistan, Israel, North Korea, Iraq, Iran, Cuba, and Serbia.

Think back to 1763 and Lord Jeffrey Amherst. He knew that sending smallpox to the Native Americans would kill hundreds of them, so he deliberately did it. This was, as we said earlier, the first example of biological warfare. Think about what smallpox did to the Aztecs or the Incas. They were virgin populations— and the disease killed millions and millions of them.

It has been over twenty years since the last naturally occurring case of smallpox. Most people who were vaccinated will no longer be immune to the disease because their vaccination will have worn out. You, your teacher, and I have never come across smallpox. Our bodies have absolutely no idea what smallpox is. We have become like the Aztecs or the Incas: We have become a virgin population.

Imagine if someone released the virus in New York City. There are over seven million people all crammed together in one place (plus all the suburbs). Say that from that initial release one person gets the disease. She gets up and gets on the subway to go to work. She passes it to everyone near her. Then she gets to the office and spreads it to everyone there. At lunchtime she spreads it to everyone in the deli. And all these people would spread it to other people. And don't forget that tourist who was standing next to the woman on the subway. He is going back home tomorrow—and he is going to give it to the people on the plane and so on. You can see what a disaster it would be. And if the disease did break out, there are two really big problems in stopping it. Most doctors would not recognize the disease. They've never studied it, and unless they knew what to look for, it would be difficult to tell it apart from more routine cases. Remember the teacher in Yugoslavia? His case was the first in that country since 1927, and so doctors

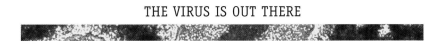

there weren't used to seeing the disease. When he turned black, they thought it was a really bad reaction to penicillin (which can sometimes have the same effect).

On top of that, there isn't enough vaccine anymore. The WHO used to have enough vaccine for 200 million people—but not anymore. In 1990, they destroyed most of it. They now have enough to protect about half a million people. And this country is not much better—we have only enough to give to seven million people. But because scientists are really worried, a program has been started to make some more—lots more—for use in an emergency.

The remaining known stocks of the smallpox virus were first scheduled to be destroyed in 1993, but destruction was delayed firstly until 1995 and then until June 30, 1999. But in May 1999, the WHO decided to delay again, until at least 2002, to allow for more research. If other countries (or even a terrorist group) have the disease, it's better we know everything we can about it, so we can better deal with it.

Maybe one day we will finally be able to completely destroy all the remaining samples of the virus—but not yet. But let's hope it will happen. Then we will truly be able to say that the most dreadful scourge of the human species, as Jenner called it, will never ever scare anyone again.

GLOSSARY

antibodies Cells in the body that attack and
kill invaders.
host The living thing in which a virus lives.
immunity State in which a living thing cannot
catch a disease because of previous exposure.
inoculation Practice of taking a mild form of a
disease and deliberately infecting a person with
it to cause immunity to the disease.
pock A scar left behind by a pustule.
pustule A growth on the skin that fills with pus
before turning into a scab.
vaccination The practice of using a vaccine.
vaccine Name given by Edward Jenner to the
matter taken from cowpox blisters and introduced into humans to provoke immunity to

smallpox. Now refers to any substance given to provoke an immune response in humans, e.g., a flu vaccine.

variola major/minor Medical names for the two types of smallpox.

virus Microscopic organism that causes infection and can live only within the cells of a host.

FOR MORE INFORMATION

In the United States

Centers for Disease Control (CDC)
1600 Clifton Road
Atlanta, GA 30333
(404) 639-3534
(800) 311-3435
Web site: http://www.cdc.gov

National Center for Infectious Diseases
See above address.
Web site: http://www.cdc.gov/ncidod

The Pan American Health Organization
Regional Office of the World Health Organization
525 Twenty-third Street NW

Washington, DC 20037
(202) 974-3000
Web site: http://www.paho.org

World Health Organization
Avenue Appia 20
1211 Geneva 27
Switzerland
Tel: (41 22) 791 21 11
Web site: http://www.who.org

In Canada

Health Canada
(Headquarters)
A.L. 0904A
Ottawa, ON K1A OK9
(613) 957-2991
Web site: http://hwcweb.hwc.ca

Office of Global Surveillance and Field Epidemiology
Health Protection Branch
Tunney's Pasture
Ottawa, ON K1A OL2
Postal Locator: 0900B

(Toronto Regional Office)
25 St. Clair Avenue East, 4th Floor
Toronto, ON M4T 1M2
(416) 973-4389

Web Sites

Epidemic!
Site based on a recent exhibition organized by the
American Museum of Natural History
http://www.amnh.org/exhibitions/epidemic

George Washington Papers
To see a scan of the original letter about inoculation
and other smallpox related letters, type "smallpox"
and "George Washington" into the search engine at
http://www.loc.gov.

World Health Organization
http://www.who.int/archives/who50/en/smallpox.htm
http://www.who.int/vaccines-diseases/history/
        history.htm

FOR FURTHER READING

DeSalle, Robert, ed. *Epidemic! The World of Infectious Diseases.* New York: New Press, 1999.

Diamond, Jared M. *Guns, Germs, and Steel: The Fates of Human Societies.* New York: W.W. Norton, 1997.

Farrell, Jeanette. *Invisible Enemies: Stories of Infectious Disease.* New York: Farrar, Straus & Giroux, 1998.

Giblin, James Cross. *When Plague Strikes: The Black Death, Smallpox, and AIDS.* New York: HarperCollins, 1995.

Karlen, Arno. *Man and Microbes: Disease and Plagues in History and Modern Times.* New York: Putnam, 1995.

Lampton, Christopher F. *Epidemic* (A Disaster! Book). Brookfield, CT: Millbrook Press, 1992.

McNeill, William H. *Plagues and Peoples*. New York: Anchor, 1989.

Ward, Brian. *Epidemic.* New York: DK Publishing, 2000.

Watts, Sheldon. *Epidemics and History: Disease, Power, and Imperialism*. New Haven, CT: Yale University Press, 1997.

Zimmerman, Barry E., and David J Zimmerman. *Killer Germs: Microbes and Diseases That Threaten Humanity*. Chicago, IL: Contemporary Books, 1996.

INDEX

CREDITS

About the Author

Tom Ridgway lives and works in Paris, France, where in 1438, smallpox killed 50,000 people.

Photo Credits

Design and Layout

Evelyn Horovicz